C000109743

LEMONADE IN THE

LEMONADE IN THE ARMENIAN QUARTER

Sarah Mnatzaganian

Published 2022 by Against the Grain Poetry Press
againstthegrainpoetrypress.wordpress.com

Author photograph by Robin Aitchison

ISBN 978-1-9163447-8-5

Printed by 4edge Limited
4edge.co.uk

Contents

To my parents

Egg Time

To my mother, Madeleine

Give me an egg, round as childhood.
I'll tap its innocent shell; push sideways
through its Humpty Dumpty head to find
a core of molten gold or the dry pollen
of a hardened heart. May this teaspoon
teach my tongue the taste of lunch hour
on a school day when I'm six, hugging
the bump under mum's dungarees.
How did the morning go? Watching her
butter home-made bread. Reading aloud
while the baby kicks. Back down the lane
for the lonely end of playtime, her love
like albumen around my ears and in
my eyes. Voices water-slow. Whistle
blown from the other side of the world.

My father taught me at night

whispering love words into the womb
while my mother slept.

He started with Armenian,
filling the mattress of my sleep
with sweet feathers:

Anoushig. Sweetheart. *Keretsig-es.*
You're beautiful. *Yes kezee
shad shad ge sirem.* I love you.

Then he spoke in West Bank Arabic
to darken my hair and make my heart
strong enough to live:

Ahlen wasahlen habibti.
May you arrive as one of the family, darling
and tread an easy path on your way.

When I heard him say *Je t'adore, ma petite,*
I pulled the thumb from my unborn mouth
to repeat each syllable.

How many ways are there to say,
I'm here. C'est moi. Who am I? Ov yem yes?
Ana khayfa. J'ai peur. *I'm afraid.*

Juice

To my father, Apraham

Every time I set spade against turf,
you're there, cutting grass-topped cliffs
into our borders, neat as the Normandy coast.

You snatch sweat from your face
and ask for *Lemon, half a lemon,*
squeezed, with water please, darling,
it quenches the thirst.

I silently sing each syllable to myself
in your voice, like no other voice,
licking the 'l' in *half* almost as long as in *lemon,*
expressing the juice of each word with your verve,
crushing the fruit's face into ridged glass
and clouding cold water with the sharpness you crave.
Each sucked finger stings.

Now I want to watch your dark throat dance
while you drink.

Made in Hemsworth

My mother has perfect ears
but she'll never know if they came
from her mum or dad.

They didn't plan to give their ears
to anyone in 1939 when the war
was young and the sacks soft

at the back of his grocery shop.
Him a married man and her
engaged to a carpenter.

Now mum knows she's one-third Viking,
she's proud of her pale and ageless skin,
her North Sea gaze.

The questioning arch of her brows
has always made her royal
in my father's eyes.

Gauguin Girls

One cradles a platter of papaya
to her bare chest and looks away
from the gaze of the sun.

Her friend holds mango blossoms
like prayer between her palms
and counsels patience.

I stop and stare. They show me
what will grow from the sore buds
on my ten-year-old chest.

Would I reach for fruit or flesh
if I were there, my fingers pale
against their warm skin?

I have no words for them,
these sisters with brown eyes.
They dare me to become woman.

You don't need to know

how many years lay between them
up on the hill fort, sun low enough
to show where ploughs scratched spelt
into chalk. How they sat on a barrow,

him in a jumper knitted by his mum,
her in a Laura Ashley dress, studying
the starved grass, harebells, yes,
and chalk-blue butterflies. Flint.

What he says next, she can't hold
in her head or take home in the hands
he never touched. What he tells her
bellies in the breeze, turns inside out
and tangles on the bullet-dented
barrow stars of Salisbury Plain.

Araxi

My aunt's comely neighbours in Jerusalem
darken their warm eyelids with kohl
before the wake at the Armenian club.

They spoon spiced coffee into a steaming pan,
watch it bubble, foam and slowly rise three times
and three times stir it back down into peace,

soothe it with sugar and fill row after row
of tiny cups to warm the mourners of Araxi, 85,
whose house the priests now claim as theirs,

steadying her hand to sign away her home
before they performed last rites. The priests sit,
bearded and beautiful, waiting for baklava

bought fresh this morning from the souk
by Araxi's daughter who leans against a wall,
pale with jetlag and a migrant's guilt.

*This poem 'Araxi' is a fictional work about imaginary characters. The
views and opinions expressed in the poem are those of the characters
only.*

Lemonade in the Armenian Quarter

Uncle Hagop planted lemon trees outside his house
where small passionate tortoises collide each spring
with the hollow *pock* of a distant tennis match.

At night his ripest lemons dropped into a crackle
of leaves. He grunted through the cardamom-coffee kitchen
into the courtyard to fill his hands with fruit.

Auntie soothed the juice with syrup and iced water.
Uncle drank, clacked his tongue and sang, *My Heart
Will Go On*, his head thrown back like a song-bird.

The lemons lay thick last February. My sister filled a bag
for Uncle. She put a smooth yellow oval into his hand
and helped him lift it to his face to smell the zest.

Dad asked the nurse for sugar and a knife. He cut,
squeezed, stirred. *See, Hagop, I'm making lemonade
from your trees.* Watched his brother smile, sip, sleep.

Der Voghormia Stp Ողորմեա (Lord have mercy on us)

To Hagop Mnatzaganian 1936-2016

You would never have allowed flowers
to frame your face, or your nostrils
to be filled with cotton wool.

You would not have borne for long
a dry wafer balanced on your lips
but would have reared up, sneezed
and thrown it on the floor.

You have left your body like a note
written on pale parchment, telling us
you are gone.

You are pared back to your core.
I never saw these wide cheekbones so uncloaked
or your generous throat lie so small and quiet
in a stiff collar and tie.

You liked to flutter your eyes and smile
when you'd argued your point
so there could be no reply.

There is no irony behind those still eyelids.
Instead, I see the moment when pain died
and you flowered in relief.

Your bright peace
teaches me how to believe
in the possibility of heaven.

Sanctuary in Dinan

A raven with a bleached head
and one blown-out umbrella wing
hops savagely round the dry church walls,
keeping to sacred ground, daring me
or anyone to take advantage of him,
flightless, legs sprung, beak bitter.

I want a quiet place to light candles.
Two euros to burn a long white taper
in memory of a friend. Four euros
for a fat candle to keep hope alight
for six hours. The taper in my hand
shakes, like the old sailor I saw

this morning, hunched on a bench,
concerned only with the safe passage
of a palsied cigarette to his lips.
It's time to go. The church warden
tells me to take my rucksack off
though I'm walking away.

Father Tree

A horse chestnut thrives on a low green mound,
its trunk like the sinewy back of my father's hand
thrust into the earth, each finger reaching
for Palestine, seeking his mother's bones.

It's spring, Dad. All the buds on every bold twig
on each gesticulating branch are shining like toffee apples
and hot cross buns – and all the birds are welcome here,
whatever language they speak.
The tree understands their need to roost.

The two candles I left burning in the cathedral
across the meadow are burning for you and for Mum
who sits by your hospital bed, watching you recover.

You're both still there, giving each other light
as I fold my hands and walk away.

Moon Mother

The moon has my mother's face
and the smile she gave when I swam
into her arms one February night.

She speaks my name cheerfully
down the phone. No hint of the time
passed since we last spoke.

I will try not to count the days
since my kids called. Imagine them walking
towards me. Bright, bright.

My mother the moon will not always
be here. She will turn her face slowly away,
profile changing, features softening.

She will deny the halo around her head
and refuse to believe her light is enough
to travel safely by.

Even moonlight makes shadows.
What else can it do? Love cannot reach
all the things it needs to touch.

Intifada Street

[The root of Intifada is Nafada: *be shaken/plumped up like a cushion*]

i.

In Jerusalem, as a boy, my father knew a peaceful street
where Munajjidoon pulled wool from tired mattresses,
washed, teased, beat it back to life and then returned it home.

Nights were soft and sleep came far more easily
when the men from Intifada Street had done their work.
What had been flattened was shaken and revived.

ii.

In his narrow Nablus shop, a baker twists filling into cakes
his family have made for no-one knows how long
in their ancient city built across two mountains.

He cooks each tambriyeh in oil and hands it to the hungry.
Solar panels glint on his roof in case the power is cut.
Rainwater sits in a dark cistern below his feet.

iii.

In Hebron, the shuttered shops rarely open their eyes.
Black nets veil the streets to trap the rubbish settlers throw
down onto their hosts. Uncle Hagop used to catch bus 231

to buy his favourite hand-blown Hebron glass: sea-blue
one year, green the next, peppered with unmelted grit,
laced with brittle bubbles of Palestinian breath.

[Munajjidoon are upholsterers.]

Auntie Merhibeh, why did we never write you down?

She never learned to read but sang her prayers
before sleep, on the sofa that was her bed;
the narrow one, just inside the front door.
A sheet, quilt and cushion for the night.

Where did she keep her clothes? How many
pieces of dry soap did she save against moths?

Her love was written on swollen knees hidden
under skirts, on bunioned feet. She was a recipe
without capitals or full stops. She knew how much salt
to sprinkle, how many days to drain the whey.

How did she make minced lamb-mint-allspice
stick to the dough of fifty lahmajoun?

She knew which old lady at Damascus Gate
sells the sweetest sage. Which corner of the kitchen
keeps the onions and garlic fresh until March.
How to banish grit from ten thousand grains of rice.

In Praise of Armenian Cooks

I cook in memory of women
who lifted heavy breasts
into the mouths of children
whose fragrant heads
were snatched from their arms
and broken against walls.

Women whose feet were shod
with horseshoes by their neighbours,
marched into wilderness, herded
into caves, pushed over cliffs.
The hairs on my back
reach out to them.

I cook in silence without sisters,
without aunts. We should be noisy
round the table, shaping pastries
on our palms for Easter, filled
with dates, walnuts, cinnamon.
Marking thorns on each edible crown.

Let's make lahmajoun, ma'loubeh.
Mince the lamb fine, grind allspice.
Melt stinking yeast with sugar
to swell the sticky dough.
Fetch cauliflower from the souk.
Our children are coming home.

Oranges for Mariam

Looking sideways like a bird listening for worms,
Ursula feels our oranges, considers the give
of their flesh, finds one soft enough
to score from pole to pole with a blunt knife.

She strips the damp petals of skin and shoves them
into her empty hot chocolate mug with absent-minded
fingers, watching Hamlet face his father's ghost
grave eyed, leaning back in her office chair.

Her great-great grandmother Mariam was married
at 13, a mother at 14. She never learned to read.
When winter blessed her son's trees in Jaffa,
she would eat no orange but his.

My father watched her part the cold segments
and lay them gently on the stove kettle's sides,
then lift them – tight with warm juice –
to her sensitive teeth, her clever tongue.

Sew up the tear

Bend over Will's torn duvet.
Send needle through cotton.

Leave the kiss of teeth
on severed thread.

Fold, press, pack him
cup, spoon, bowl him

soap, pepper, salt him
list, gather, kiss him

hold and release him.

Food Run

She knocks back her latte like a seal gulping mackerel
and heads for the station with gifts for her first-born:

Eucalyptus leaves to fill his room with forest medicine,
fresh goat's cheese, a green-gold throw for his college chair,

a bottle of colloidal silver to murder the germs in his throat.
FLANNERY, scoffs a crane by the tracks.

A round cake of apples and almonds, a Guernsey sweater,
heavily darned, and two letters from the bank. She might arrive

with nothing to say. At the bottom of her trolley: Ribston Pippin,
Adams Pearmain, Blenheim Orange, Winter Gold.

The cake was still warm when she packed it last night. It may
have ripened the apples a little. She should have made pesto.

Cake Again

When there's no way to touch
or give anything but words

it's time to reach for butter eggs
spice syrup honey nuts apricots,

to melt-stir-beat myself into a bowl
and ask what more to add of zest

or juice to his tomorrow. Perhaps
the gentleness of chocolate would

say it better, moist enough not
to stick in his throat, wrapped

noisily in foil, nosed into a jiffy bag.
Cake again? the post office lady says.

It costs more to send than make.
More to let go than hold.

Ursula

Sixteen years, eight months and ten days later
she puts her head on my lap
and becomes very still,
lips closed; life expressed
in the twitch of a shoulder,
the gleam of eyelids.

Her forehead is Armenian,
jaw and eyes Jewish,
mouth and nose pure English rose.

The side zips of her dungarees
grin tightly round her hips with shiny,
square teeth and she's narrowed her shirt
to skim soft sides.

I will not be afraid.
I will not be afraid when she wakes
and walks away.

Philosophy Revision

We take flashcards for a walk
as if she's not really revising,

as if all we wanted
was the comfort of trees at twilight,

as if success wasn't
a passport to somewhere else.

Dusk deepens our eyes
and the distance to the ground is hard to judge.

I drain my mind to a dry riverbed
and wait for her monsoon to flood me

with what I will know for only as long
as she needs me to know it.

For only as long as it takes to leave.

Uncle Hagop in Stratford-upon-Avon

I'm on a camp site by the river,
wading through the flood that followed rain
where, undeterred, Uncle Hagop swims upstream.

His joy buoys him up like Dead Sea water.
Floating head and shoulders high, he walruses
his favourite lines:

Now is the winter of our discontent

Tomorrow and tomorrow and tomorrow

If music be the food of love

He's in his element, twice.
Swans gather in his wake, curling respectful necks.
We leave our sodden tents and follow.

Grain Culture Bakery, March 2020

We obey the pavement's pink chalk stripes,
two metres apart. We check our phones
to pass the time – or pitch a few words underarm,
like soft tennis balls, to the next in line.

It's easy, talking to strangers, these strange days.
Something has loosened our tongues.
Not just our shared desire for cardamom twists
and seeded sourdough. Greedy for more

than bagels and bostock, we wait outside,
grateful to stand in sanctioned sunlight
and breathe the air. I groan at the scent
of fresh bread from the open door.

Behind me, a man asks, *What can you smell?*
Croissants, brioche, hot cross buns, I say,
but that's not all. What I smell is sweet
as a baby's head after sleep, soft as its feet.

It's fresh as the blackbird's steady serenade
this Saturday morning on St Mary's Street.
I smell the small warm realities we can tuck
under one arm and take, contented, home.

Company of Trees

Each poplar, lime, ash, oak, says
my people are not far away.

We're gathered close enough, a bird
can sing from one, be heard by all.

Close enough for our roots to meet, talk,
feed each other, warn of disease.

Come, everyone I love! Let's feel
the same roar of rain on our branches.

See each other's faces change
with every day of spring.

We'll caterpillar the grass with catkins
and shed silver bark without pain.

Let's grow new arms from our sawn trunks.
Unleash from our black bark

flowers of white, then rain-crushed pink,
our canopies triumphant, complete.

Green Valley Supermarket

I've come to gather Lebanese olives,
babaghanoush, fresh yellow dates, labane,
baby cucumbers, pitta bread, ma'moul
and the cardamom nougat they call Manna.

I try to tell the staff my dad taught Arabic
to the owner's sons, but they don't understand.
I want them to know I'm here to buy
the flavours of my father's childhood.

I'm looking for the foods his mother Takouhi
first fed her youngest son, smiling as he kissed
her neck and kissed again until she laughed
and shooed him, *Ahbel! Silly boy!*

When he wakes from his operation today,
as his mother did not; when he wakes,
as she could not, without a clot in his veins;
when he's home, safely stitched, meshed, glued;

when he sits with us as she never did again
we can tear good bread, pour oil, sprinkle salt
and watch him close his eyes to the smoke
of aubergine, the sharpness of strained yoghurt.

Morning

I had a Gretel moment back there, thinking I'd lost my way,
until I spotted yellow poplar leaves spattering the path
and knew I'd seen them before,

surprised by their bright circles against the mud
on my way through Shropshire rain,
early this late-August morning.

Nearly home, I join a congregation of trees
at the head of the valley. They have no book.
They're here to breathe, drink light and listen.

From time to time, a motherly dove or dark rook speaks.
Wind sends quiet applause through the leaves of oak and ash
and the sun bowls light straight down the valley.

I would give this morning to those I don't even love,
whom I've never met,
who are not yet born.

Acknowledgements

Warm thanks to the editors of the magazines where many of these poems were first published, including *The North, The Rialto, 14 Magazine, Fenland Reed, Ink Sweat and Tears, Poetry News, Atrium, Pennine Platform, As Above, So Below* and *Poetry and Covid. Egg Time* was a prizewinner in the Winter 2020 Poetry Society competition on the theme of 'Youth', judged by Phoebe Power.

Thank you to Avril Bruton, my college tutor, for telling me I could write, and to Jonathan Hopkinson, for believing my work would find its way into print. Thanks to my best friend, biographer Midge Gillies, for insisting I attend an Arvon course in 2015, and perennial thanks to the tutors on that course, Peter and Ann Sansom of The Poetry Business, who have been generous mentors and friends ever since. Helena Nelson of Happenstance Press: thank you for your unstinting honesty and support. Wendy Cope has cast her clear eyes over my work for the last six years; I can't thank her enough. Thanks too to Poetry School seminar tutors Moniza Alvi and Heidi Williamson and all the poets I workshop with regularly, especially the *Nearly Northern Collective* who have been a solace and inspiration almost every Saturday morning since the first lockdown. Especial thanks to poet Paul Stephenson for suggesting the title of this pamphlet and for his laser-sharp insight. Thank you, my wonderful family, for your love and faith.

Abegail Morley, thank you for being the kindest and most patient of editors who, along with Karen Dennison and Jessica Mookherjee, decided that this book deserved publication by the exceptional Against The Grain Poetry Press.